AF544967

Set design by Jeff Cowie *Photo by Jim Caldwell*

(Left to right) Jean Stapleton, Roberta Maxwell and Hallie Foote in a scene from The Alley Theatre production of *The Carpetbagger's Children.*

THE CARPETBAGGER'S CHILDREN

BY HORTON FOOTE

DRAMATISTS PLAY SERVICE INC.

In memory of my wife Lillian Vallish Foote.

THE CARPETBAGGER'S CHILDREN received its world premiere at the Alley Theatre (Gregory Boyd, Artistic Director; Paul R. Tetreault, Managing Director) in Houston, Texas, on June 1, 2001. It was directed by Michael Wilson; the set design was by Jeff Cowie; the lighting design was by Rui Rita; the sound design and original music were by John Gromada; the costume design was by David Woolard; and the stage manager was Amy Knotts. The cast was as follows:

CORNELIA .... Roberta Maxwell
GRACE ANNE .... Jean Stapleton
SISSIE .... Hallie Foote

The Alley Theatre production of the THE CARPETBAGGER'S CHILDREN was subsequently presented by the Hartford Stage Company (Michael Wilson, Artistic Director) in Hartford, Connecticut, on September 6, 2001.

The Alley Theatre production was then presented by the Guthrie Theater (Joe Dowling, Artistic Director; Susan Baird Trapnell, Managing Director) in Minneapolis, Minnesota, on August 3, 2001.

The Alley Theatre production received its New York City premiere at Lincoln Center Theater (André Bishop, Artistic Director; Bernard Gersten, Managing Director) on March 25, 2002.

CHARACTERS

CORNELIA

GRACE ANNE

SISSIE

PLACE

Harrison, Texas.

TIME

The present.

THE CARPETBAGGER'S CHILDREN

The stage is in darkness. The lights are slowly brought up. At three corners of the stage are chairs. In each chair is one of the Thompson girls: Cornelia, Grace Anne and Sissie. Cornelia is looking at a ledger book and writing in figures, Grace Anne is sewing and Sissie sits in silence. In the center of the stage is a table with many family pictures on it and four chairs placed around it. In the distance we hear dance music. As the lights are brought up on Cornelia's area she is going over accounts in a ledger book.

CORNELIA. Hear that music? That is from the Opera House. They're having a dance there tonight. Whenever I hear dance music I think of Beth. She loved to dance. I never learned to dance. Grace Anne danced and Sissie but Beth was the loveliest dancer I ever saw. Beth was Papa's favorite when she was alive, no question about that. Mama's too. Mine. Brother's. We all adored her. She went away one winter to visit some cousins in St. Louis and stayed seven months. We missed her so — let her stay as long as she wants, Papa said, she's having a good time. She deserves it. We were such a happy family then it seemed to me. Papa's closest friend was Colonel Hawkins. He lived next door and had been Captain in the Confederate Army. Beth used to say, Look the War is over for sure now, here comes Papa and Colonel Hawkins walking home together again, talking away. They'd walk up to the sidewalk leading to our house. Stop and talk and talk and talk. And then still talking they'd walk to the sidewalk leading to his house, stand there and talk and talk. Until Mrs. Hawkins would send one of her girls out with some excuse to get Colonel Hawkins into the house because she couldn't stand that Colonel Hawkins and Papa were best friends. You see Mrs. Hawkins was doing all she could to keep the Confederacy alive here. And the Colonel still had a plantation not five miles out from Harrison. And Papa, well, much to my shame when I was growing up, had come to Texas with the Union Army and had liked what he saw so much that he decided to come on back here after the War during reconstruction to live. Anyway, that's the story we were brought up on. However it was, when he got here again things were in chaos, the slaves were all freed, and the plantation owners couldn't hold onto their land, and Papa, being one of the few white Republicans here then, had been appointed County Treasurer and Tax Collector which enabled him to know first on who couldn't pay their taxes. And, according to Papa, Colonel Hawkins was about to lose his plantation. And Jenkins, another white man and a Republican, came to Papa and said, I hear Colonel Hawkins can't pay his taxes and may have to give up his land. I want it. I want you to find a way to raise the taxes on his land so he won't for sure be able to pay them, so I can get hold of it. Papa refused and went to Colonel Hawkins and told him what Jenkins was up to and Colonel Hawkins got together with some of his friends and called on Jenkins that night and told him if he stayed in town another day he would be killed. That frightened Jenkins and he left town for good. Colonel Hawkins was able to pay his taxes and that year he made a wonderful cotton crop and he decided to move his family off the plantation and into town and bought a vacant lot next to us and built his house. I don't know whether it was his friendship or something in Papa's character that made people here forgive Papa for being in the Union Army, a Republican and a Carpetbagger. Grace Anne said they never did forgive him, they tolerated him because of his friendship with Colonel Hawkins. But that's Grace Anne for you. She always had to be different from the rest of us. I think she always resented the fact that Beth was Papa's favorite. Mama's too. Mine. Everybody's. And then Grace Anne was not pretty. Not plain exactly but not ever pretty. Sissie wasn't really a beauty either, but she was always so sweet, had the disposition of a saint, born that way, that you didn't really care what she looked like. But Beth was beautiful. And that wasn't just my opinion. Everybody in town thought so. She was beautiful and she was stylish. And Beth was the big Boss of the family, too, you know. Even Papa asked her opinion about things. And then she got sick. We called in all the doctors here. Dr. Valls and Dr. Andrews and Dr. Davidson and they all examined her and consulted among themselves and said they didn't know what was wrong and Papa had better take her to a specialist and so I went with him and we took her to New Orleans and Papa spent a fortune on Doctors and whatever it was, we never really understood, they said it couldn't be cured and we were going to lose her, and Papa thanked them and said I'll take her home then, and Beth thought she was cured and that's why she was going home, and we didn't tell her anything different but she couldn't understand why if she was cured and able to go home she couldn't walk and still had to stay on her berth all the way home. Colonel Hawkins had arranged for a number of the men in town to meet our train and they carried Beth off the train to a wagon they had waiting for her and lifted her onto the wagon and Papa said to me, look they have covered the streets with straw so she will have a smooth ride to our house, and because of the straw there were no ruts to jar the wagon as we took her home. The men carried her up the stairs to her room, and the street in front of our house was covered with straw every day the whole time she was sick, so that the wagons and the horses passing the house went by as silently as humanly possible. And we all prayed day and night for God to make her well. Grace Anne praying the loudest of all. I could hear her praying in the next room to mine. Dear God, take me, but spare our dear sister Beth. But none of our prayers did any good and she died three weeks after we brought her home, thinking all the time she was going to get well. She died at two o'clock in the morning. Papa was sitting up with her bathing her face with a cold cloth and I heard him sob and I went to him and he was holding her sobbing. We've lost Beth, he said over and over. We've lost Beth. A week after her funeral Papa called me into his room and asked me to shut the door and I did and he said, Cornelia I'm turning to you now that Beth is gone. Your brother means well, but he hasn't a lot of common sense, nor does Grace Anne or Sissie — sweet and loveable all of them in their own way and I feel blessed in having them, but I don't think any of them are ready for any kind of responsibility. And so now that Beth is gone I'm turning to you, so if anything happens to me you will know what to do. And beginning tomorrow I will take you each day to one of the cotton farms and tell you what I paid for it and what it's worth now and who are good and responsible tenants and who's not. And he did. Every afternoon for a month he would come home early, hitch up the buggy and off we'd go. Brother and Sissie would go along sometimes, too, but never Grace Anne. He would ask her, but she would always pretend she had something else to do. Slipping off and seeing Jackson Le Grand we found out later. At night Papa would go over his books with me. What the taxes on the land were, what arrangements he had with this tenant and what arrangements he had with that tenant. And one night he said to me, Cornelia. I'm concerned about your Brother. I worry if he doesn't have something to do, something to give him a sense of responsibility, he'll never amount to anything. Snyder's Dry Good Store is up for sale and I'm thinking of buying it for your Brother. What do you think of that idea? I said I thought it was a good one, and that's what Papa did. Bought Mr. Snyder's Dry Good Store and put Brother in charge. And at first it all went well. Then Mr. Snyder did a sneaky thing and opened another store just down the street and took away most of Brother's customers. We heard from friends that he was referring to Brother's store as the Carpetbagger's store, but when Papa went to him about that he denied he ever said it. *(The music is heard again.)* Beth told me once when she was so sick, when I get out of this bed I'm going to teach you to dance, but of course she never got well and I never learned. *(She goes back to her ledger book as the lights fade and are brought up on Grace Anne seated in a rocker sewing on a dress.)*

GRACE ANNE. Poor Brother. Papa bought a Dry Goods Store for him, a chicken hatchery, a Studebaker car dealership and they all failed. And he worked hard, too, didn't drink, was responsible and tended to business, but he didn't prosper. Someone said to me once, Grace Anne, nothing your brother touches prospers does it? And it certainly seemed that way. So, after Papa died, he just gave up and quit trying. Stayed home all the time. Cornelia pretended he was helping her and he would ride out to the farms with her and inspect the crops, but she never let him near the books or write out a single check. I knew that for a fact, because once when Brother got mad at her, he came over to my house complaining, but I said what can I do Brother? I have no authority at all. Lost that the day I married. Oh, I knew about Brother and his mistress, that mulatto woman Hessie Gallagher. She made the dress I'm wearing right now. Yes. She did. It's almost fifteen years old this dress, and she made it. She was the best dressmaker I've ever known and the town has ever known. She lived across the tracks just two blocks behind the icehouse, and I want you to know she lived in a nice house, always freshly painted, neat yard, lovely flowers. All you needed to do was to get to T. Gordon's or Schwartzes store and pick out a pattern you liked and take it to Hessie and say Hessie can you have this for me in a week, and she'd say, Yes, Ma'am and she'd have it for you too. And when she died last year I went to her funeral with five friends of mine, all customers of hers. We were the only white people there. I don't know why Brother gave her up. I never could figure if Hessie knew either, but whatever it was, it didn't seem to affect her one way or the other, for we'd always greet each other the same and spend a few minutes talking about the weather and the price of things and then I'd show her my patterns and sometimes she'd suggest a few improvements or sometimes she'd say I think you should keep it just as it is. Once in a while, after Papa died, I would go see Mama. And Mama by this time had started getting all mixed up in her mind, and every time I'd go over to see her, which was at the most every two months or so, she'd start hollering to the help or my sisters or anyone around at the time. Get her out of here, I know what she's come for. She's trying to trap Brother into marrying her, just like the rest of the women in this town. I'm on to them — they come over here you know and I say what do you want? And they say we're here to play bridge with Sissie or Cornelia, and I say like hell you are. Like hell you are. You're not here to play bridge with nobody. You're here after Brother. And my sisters would say, Mama do you know who that is? That's Grace Anne. Your daughter Grace Anne and she has come to see you and I wanted to say,

Mama, you're wasting your breath because Brother has never been interested in white women, that was before Mrs. Carpenter of course. Once he started going with her they were inseparable. He could take her everyplace because she was white. The only place he couldn't take her was his own house, because Mama would have a fit when she'd see them together and start screaming, get that hussy out of here, she is trying to trap Brother, and poor Mrs. Carpenter would have to leave. Well, I have to make my own dresses now. I couldn't afford Hessie now if she were alive. If my luck doesn't change soon I may have to start sewing for other people too. How come my Brother and Sisters are rich and I'm not? Well, that's a long story. They never made any more money than I did. Papa made it all, made it in a hurry too, my friends used to whisper to me. You see Papa was a Union Soldier sent to Texas and when the War was over he liked it so well around here, he decided to come on back. Anyway, that's Mama's story. People in town have another story which I was told often enough by so-called friends in school. He was sent here as a part of the Reconstruction when the Yankees took over the county and the courthouse and got himself appointed County Treasurer and Tax Collector and when the plantations were breaking up and people couldn't pay their taxes, he grabbed land right and left and held onto it. When I was growing up I always dreaded the day in school when the Civil War would come up and somebody would point to me and say, as if it had never been said before, her Papa was a Carpetbagger. Anyway, like Mama once said, money stopped that kind of talk once it had been established Papa was a rich Carpetbagger and nobody was ever going to take the land or his money away from him. The one thing I remember most about my Papa was calling us to him just before we said our prayers and making us promise we would never, ever sell or divide a piece of the land he had gotten together. And everyone kept that promise too, everybody except me. And they've never in their hearts forgiven me for that, and I don't think they ever will. Mama and Papa never wanted us to marry, you know. None of us. Not only Brother, but none of us girls. They thought everybody was after our land and our money. Well I defied them and eloped with Jackson Le Grand, and when Papa heard what I'd done, he and

Brother were after us to stop us, but we'd taken the train to Victoria and got married there in the parlor of a cousin of Jackson's, so by the time Brother and Papa found out where we were it was too late to stop us. He sent word to where we were honeymooning not to bother ever to come home again with or without my husband, and I never did while Papa was alive. When Papa died I asked Jackson if he'd go with me to the funeral and he said no, he didn't want me around when he was alive and I've no interest in going now he's dead. So I wrote Mama a note saying I would like to come and say goodbye to Papa and it was Cornelia that called me on the phone and said I could come, but without Jackson, so I went to the house, to the church and to the cemetery, sat with the family at the church and at the cemetery and when it was all over I asked if I could go back to the house with them, and they said yes. Brother and I weren't speaking by then, he'd made a remark about Jackson uptown the day after Papa died that was repeated to me and I called him up and I said, Brother, did you say uptown yesterday that Jackson had married me for my money? Yes, I did, he said. Because I think it's true, so does everybody else in town. What money? I said, I don't have a dime to my name and you know it. But he's counting on the future. What future? I asked. The day Mama dies and the Estate is divided. That's a lie and you know it, I said. Jackson married me for love and nothing else. I bet, he said. Well, you can just march back downtown, I said and tell everyone you have told that lie to that it's a lie, or I'll never speak to you again. Suit yourself, he said, suit yourself. When I told Jackson later on what Brother said, he said, well, you will be rich one day. There's nothing wrong with that. Just be sure you're smart and look out for what is coming to you, because your Papa's gone now and Beth and so there's only Sissie and Cornelia and Brother and your Mama. I know when your Mama goes. What are you talking about? I said. When Mama goes? When she dies. Your Papa left everything in her name, when she dies who is she leaving it to? I don't think she's leaving it to anybody. I just think the Estate will be kept together and we will live off the proceeds. Who will? We all will, I said. Are you getting any of it now? He asked. No. I had to admit. And I don't want any of it, as long as Brother and I are not speaking and you're not allowed to come ouse. And I was happy, too, married to Jackson. From the rt we were happy. There was one rough time for us when t baby died, and I was told I couldn't have any more children. I sent for Mama then and asked her to please come and see me as I knew Papa would never allow me to come to the house to see her and I needed comforting. And she defied Papa for once in her life and came to where we were living and even spoke to Jackson. She sent me a check a week later she said to help with the funeral expenses incurred at the time of the death of the baby. Then to the surprise of the doctor, I got pregnant again and had Lily Beth and Dolores Susan. Those days Jackson had a job at the cotton gin, making very little, I might add. Then Mr. Carson who ran the cotton gin replaced him with his son, and there were no other jobs in sight just then and Jackson said to me one day, after Papa died, you know I think I'll try farming. I think I could make a go of that. What are you going to farm? I asked. Well, honey, he said, you know you'll one day have a share of a very large Estate. Some said uptown yesterday your Mama was left twenty thousand acres by your Papa. Now your share will be, when it's divided, at least five thousand acres. When will that be? I said. When your Mama dies. Stop talking about Mama dying, I said. She could live a long, long time. She could, he said. She could. And it turned out I was right. She did live a long, long time. *(She goes back to her sewing as the lights fade. The lights are brought up on Sissie's area. She sings "Mighty Lak a Rose." The songs that are heard during the play are sometimes to be prerecorded and sometimes sung live. When Sissie finishes singing she turns to the audience.)*

SISSIE. I'm the baby. I always liked being the baby. I liked being told what to do, and what not to do, what to think and what not to think. My daughter got mad at me once and said Sissie, she always called me Sissie, never Mama, Sissie I don't think you have ever had a thought or an opinion of your own. Ever. I expect that's right. When Grace Anne married Jackson Le Grand I thought to myself I could never do anything like that. Never upset Papa or Mama or my sister like that. I had such a happy childhood. Roberta Thatcher was my best friend and lived just down the street and whenever it rained, and it rained a lot, Roberta would bring her paper dolls over here and we would play paper dolls all day up in our attic. I had a cousin too, Lenora, that would come over and play with me. But she had such a sad life, so different from mine. She married Leon Davis just out of high school and her Papa and Mama left here and moved to Houston and she and Mr. Davis went soon after. We didn't stay in touch much but I knew things weren't going well for them, because her Papa, my Uncle Joe, Mama's brother, came twice to try and borrow money from Cornelia and Cornelia felt she had to say no, and then there was some property Mama was left that Uncle Joe said he should have had a share of and he sued Mama about that and he lost, and then he stopped speaking to us, and the next thing we heard was that Lenora had left Leon and taken their three children and had moved in with her Mama and Papa and then we read in the Houston paper that Leon had shot Uncle Joe, in self-defense he told reporters, because Uncle Joe had tried to stab him with a butcher knife. Which I didn't believe because I always thought Uncle Joe was kind and gentle, but I kept my opinion to myself because the rest of the family was still mad at Uncle Joe because he had sued us. Anyway, where was I? *(In the distance we hear a child faintly singing "Jesus Loves Me." It should be prerecorded.)* Oh, yes. About playing paper dolls on rainy afternoons. And about that time I found out I had a sweet singing voice. It was Mrs. Payne at Sunday School who heard me singing. *(Sissie joins in singing along with the recording of the child singing "Jesus Loves Me.")* And she called up Mama and said Sissie has a sweet singing voice and I'd love to have her study singing with me, and Mama asked me if I wanted to and I said yes, as long as I didn't have to sing before anyone, because I would be terrified to stand up in the choir like Miss Agnes Treat and sing a solo, and Mama said no one will ever make you do that if you don't want to, so I went once a week and studied singing, and finally I got so I could sing before Papa and Mama and Brother and Cornelia at the house. Papa's favorites were "Just a Song at Twilight" and "After the Ball." And pretty soon I got to singing around town. I sang at the Methodist Washington Birthday Tea, three years in a row, and I sang, "Oh, Promise Me" at Judy Gaylord's wedding, and I was going to sing "The Broken Link" at Hester Galbraith's funeral, but I became so emotional looking at her coffin while I was singing that I began to sob and cry in the middle of the song and Cornelia had to come and lead me out of the church. No one ever asked me to sing at a funeral after that. It was about this time I met Ralph Goodman. He asked if he could call on me and I asked Cornelia what she thought and she talked it over with Mama, and Mama said it would be all right as long as he didn't try to take me for a walk at night or to the picture show, and so he came over one Sunday night after church and he asked me to sing for him and I sang "Waltz Me Around Again Willie" and he asked if we had a Victrola and I said we did and he said do you think your Mama would mind if we danced? And I said have you forgotten this is Sunday? We don't dance here in this house on Sunday, and he said, Oh, forgive me I forgot. I was so taken with you, I forgot what day it was. Well, he kept coming over and Mama gave us permission to dance as long as she or Cornelia were in the room and one night he told me he loved me and would I marry him? And I began to cry then and he said what's the matter? And I said I can't marry you and he said why not, don't you like me? And I said I do, and he said I love you, do you think you could ever love me? And I said I don't know. Maybe. And he said if you found out one day you loved me would you marry me then? And I said no and he said why not? And I said well, because of what Grace Anne did. She eloped with Jackson Le Grand and Papa never spoke to her again. And he said he wasn't talking about eloping he wanted to get married in a church before God and I said Mama wouldn't ever say yes to that because Papa didn't want any of us ever to marry and he said let me ask and see what she says to me, because I'm not Jackson Le Grand. I'm a go-getter and I'm going to get a fine job in Houston, which I can't discuss yet, and I want to take you with me. Oh, I couldn't do that I said, I'd miss my family living in Houston and he said just give it a try and if you don't like Houston we'll come back here. And can we live here with Mama? I asked. Oh, I don't think that would be practical he said, but we could live near them and Mama came in then and he said may I speak to you about a very serious matter? And she said yes and they went into the next room and he asked if we could marry and she called in Cornelia and Brother and asked their opinion and Cornelia said it was all right with her as long as Ralph Goodman would sign a paper never asking that the

Estate be divided as that was the wish of Papa and he said he had no interest in the Estate and they called me in then and told me I could get married, and we got married in the Methodist Church, and I asked Grace Anne to be my matron of honor but she refused as she said she'd had to elope and not been spoken to for a number of years after that. Anyway, it was a lovely wedding and I moved to Houston, but I missed my family so that Ralph said that I could come back here and live with Mama and he would come out every other weekend to be with me as his job in Houston was too important to leave, and that's what I did and that's what he does. He comes out every other weekend. And so I keep happy and whenever I get discouraged I just sing to myself one of the songs I used to sing in Sunday School. *Sissie sings "Brighten the Corner Where You Are." (As she is seated in her chair the lights on her fade and are brought up on Cornelia's area.)*

CORNELIA. I wasn't with Papa when he died I'm sorry to say. Colonel Hawkins had died the year before and Papa, I believe, never got over missing him. He stopped walking to town soon after Colonel Hawkins died and closed his office in town and moved his office to our house. Papa was talking about Beth all the time now. She would have been almost forty if she had lived and he worried about Grace Anne, although he still wouldn't speak to her, and had me inquire from friends of hers how they were getting along. By the hardest, I was told. They were living in a rented room at Mrs. Taylor's house. When Papa heard that he said let's start giving Grace Anne, not a penny for her husband, but Grace Anne a hundred dollars a month as her share of the profits from the Estate, that way I'll know she won't starve. He sent me over to talk to her and take a check, but she refused the help. Well, we tried he said. I'll live to see the day she'll be coming here begging for help. But he never did, of course, he died before that ever happened. He wasn't sick at all, you know. He and I had been out to one of the farms to see how the cotton crops looked and when he came home he went into the parlor and called Sissie to come and sing for him. And Sissie asked if she could call her friend Roberta Thatcher to accompany her on the piano and Papa said no, just sing all by yourself. Mama and brother joined us then. And Sissie sang five songs for him and then he said would she sing,

"Marching Through Georgia"? And she said she didn't want to sing that, and he said why not? And she said because Sherman was vile and a beast and did terrible things to the South and he said who told her that? And she said I heard it at the meeting of the United Daughters of the Confederacy and he said do you go to the United Daughters of the Confederacy? And she said I only went once with my friend Roberta Thatcher. And he turned to Mama and said do you know about this? And Mama said no, it's the first I've heard about it, and Sissie began crying again and said she was sorry and would never go again and Papa said she was forgiven and for Sissie to stop crying, and she said she would, and she sang "Marching Through Georgia" then and I felt ashamed of myself, but I was hoping none of our friends would come in just then, because I knew how all of them felt about Sherman, and Papa said when she finished that to show how broad-minded he was he would like her to sing "Dixie" and she did and we all joined in singing it with her, including Papa and Brother, and then Sissie started crying then and when Papa asked her what the matter was she said she missed our Sister Beth and we all started crying then, even Papa and Brother, and Mama went and got Beth's picture which none of us felt did her justice, but it was the only picture we had and the next morning he called me into his office and said he wanted to let me look at his Will which he had just drawn up and I read it and saw that the Estate was going to be left to Mama, under certain conditions, that it was to never be divided under any circumstances and that the proceeds from the Estate were to be distributed equally to each of us including Grace Anne and I was always to be in charge of the Estate. Mama asked us to dinner then, and Papa told me to go on without him, he was tired and thought he would take a nap and then he asked me to have Sissie come into his room and sing to him, as her singing soothed him, and she went in and I could hear her singing Papa's favorite hymn, "O, the Clanging Bells of Time." *(We hear Cornelia's memory of Sissie singing "O, the Clanging Bells of Time." It should be prerecorded.)* And then I went into the dining room and Mama and I listened to Sissie singing, then Mama began saying Grace, the only prayer she knew. Then we heard screaming, screaming like I've never heard anyone scream before and we all went running up the stairs to Papa's bedroom and Sissie was beside his bed screaming, and I looked at Papa on the bed and I said, my God, Mama, Papa is dead and she began to scream then and the cook heard us screaming and came up to see what the matter was and she saw Papa dead and she started to scream too. Brother went right away for Doctor Valls and I was trying to comfort Mama and Sissie and Louisa, the cook, when Brother came in with Dr. Valls and when I saw Dr. Valls I began to cry and Brother began to cry too and Dr. Valls looked at Papa and said you're right, son, he is dead I'm sorry to say and the town has lost a fine man. Well, I got hold of myself then and said to Brother go to Mr. Ross' funeral home and have him come for Papa. When would you like the funeral? Brother said and I said heavens that depends on so much. Like what? He said. Well, what if Papa's cousins that live in St. Louis, that Beth spent seven months with, want to come? How long would it take them to get here? It turned out they couldn't come, sent a lovely wire of condolences and flowers. And everybody in town was so nice. I never saw so much food as was sent over. Anyway in the late afternoon of the day Papa died Brother went to the Post Office and came home with a letter to Mama from Grace Anne wanting to come to the funeral and we talked it over and Mama told me to call her and say she was welcome to come without Jackson. Which I did and she thanked me and said she would be with us and to give her love to Mama. And she told someone later that Jackson wouldn't have come even if he had been asked, as he was very resentful still at the treatment shown him by Papa. Anyway, she came and we made her welcome and it was my duty after the funeral to explain to her about the Will and that she was to share in whatever the Estate made after certain expenses were deducted and she said.

GRACE ANNE. *(Speaking from the chair.)* What expenses?

CORNELIA. Well, I was to get a salary as I had for some time.

GRACE ANNE. *(Speaking from the chair.)* For what?

CORNELIA. I was going to manage the Estate and Papa specified in his Will that I was going to be paid for that.

GRACE ANNE. *(Getting up from her chair.)* How much?

CORNELIA. Two hundred dollars a month.

GRACE ANNE. Mercy, that's a fortune. Why that's more than

Jackson Le Grand makes at the cotton gin keeping their books.

CORNELIA. *(Turning away from Grace Anne.)* Well, I almost answered her back, but I said to myself, Cornelia consider the source she has always been jealous-hearted. *(Turning to Grace Anne.)* How did you like Brother Graham's eulogy for Papa?

GRACE ANNE. All right I guess, but why did he have to bring up that he was from the North and a Union Soldier?

CORNELIA. Because that's what he was. *(Again turnng away from Grace Anne.)* Although I wished in my heart he hadn't made so much of it either. And Mrs. Cotman came in looking for me then and began to cry when she saw us together and she said, Oh, thank God the rift in your family has been healed and you two have forgiven each other. *(Grace Anne gives Cornelia a look and goes back to her chair.)* It was Brother that warned me we'd be having trouble with Grace Anne. We knew that the day she eloped to marry Jackson Le Grand, whose family had nothing, and who had only, just piddly jobs around town, she'd be poor as anything. Anyway, Brother said don't tell Mama or Sissie but Grace Anne and Jackson Le Grand are inquiring about how many acres we have. Why? I said. Because I'll bet you every dollar I have she is going to ask to divide it up and give her her share now. Mama will never do it, I said. Never in this world. I know she won't. What are you all whispering about? Mama said. Let me in on the secret. Oh, nothing, Mama, nothing at all. Then Mama said, as if we had never been told before, Beth is dead. Been dead for ten years. And that's when we started worrying about Mama's forgetting. That's one thing though she never forgot, no matter in the years to come how mixed up she was. She announced every now and again, Beth is dead. Beth is dead. Been dead for ten years. And no matter how we tried to tell her and say, Mama, Beth has been dead fifteen years or twenty, she would insist on it being ten. Anyway, it wasn't long before we had to tell Mama and Sissie what Grace Anne and her husband were up to. They'd hired a lawyer and he came to us and demanded to see a copy of Papa's Will and was telling all over town a great injustice had been done his client, our sister, and that a lot of the Estate had been gotten under very cloudy circumstances during the Reconstruction and that he was going to look into that part of it too. Well, we didn't know what to do, hire a lawyer for ourselves or to go to Grace Anne and plead with her to call off her trifling husband and reason with her that she is to share in the profits from the Estate, and finally I made Sissie go see her and she didn't stay long but came back and said Grace Anne wanted nothing except what she had been told by her lawyer was rightfully hers and what's that? I asked and Sissie said a fourth of the land and a fourth of all the assets including our house. Well, she's some kind of fool I said if she thinks I will ever let her have that. I'll burn the house down first, I'll … then Brother said calm down Sister, that's just that lawyer getting her to talk that way, I would try to settle it. How? I said. Make them an offer he said. Like what? I said. I would offer them ten thousand in cash and five hundred acres of land. Do you think they would settle for that? All I know, he said, is Jackson Le Grand is out of work and they owe everybody in town including the grocery store. Well, try it, I said and see what happens. I can't go to Grace Anne, he said. We're not speaking. Are you speaking to Jackson? I said. I guess, he said, at least we were yesterday morning. I passed him uptown and he said good morning and I said good morning. Well, go talk to him, I said and he did and came back and said he'll settle for fifteen thousand in cash and a thousand acres of land. My God, I said, he's greedy. Didn't I warn you, Brother said. Well, go back and tell him we'll give him twelve thousand dollars and seven hundred and fifty acres of land. And by five o'clock that afternoon it was a done deal. We had our lawyer draw up the papers and Mama sign them and we had Jackson off our backs. And they lived pretty high there for awhile, but Jackson was no cotton farmer and the next thing we heard he was borrowing money from the bank. It took him ten years, but he finally lost all the land to the bank but they did get a house out of it. Bought one for three thousand dollars out of the money we gave them. When we heard the bank had taken over the land we had given them I was upset and said I want to buy our land back and I did, so we owned once again all the land Papa had left. Jackson is dead now and Grace Anne and her girls live on in the house they bought. She gets by somehow. She gave up all rights and income from the Estate when we gave Jackson the land and the money, and she's never asked us for anything since Jackson died. We send the girls money to buy dresses for special occasions like high school graduation and every change of season we tell them to go to a store in town where we have a charge account and get clothes. And we send Grace Anne money as a present on her birthdays, at first she sent it back, but we just kept sending it anyway and lately she's been keeping it. She comes over, every now and again now and visits with us. Last Easter she and the girls came over for dinner. The girls are sweet and friendly and come over quite often. Now that Sissie has her baby girl, they seem just crazy about their cousin. Grace Anne sent Sissie a baby gift too when her little girl was born. *(The lights fade on Cornelia's area and are brought up on Sissie's area.)*

SISSIE. I was sitting on the gallery with Mama when Leon Davis who had been married to my cousin Lenora and had shot and killed her father he said in self-defense and had been acquitted, appeared one day. He said he was just riding through Harrison as he had been to Victoria on business and saw us sitting on the porch and decided to stop by and say hello. Cornelia and Brother had gone out to look at the farms that morning. I told him that, and he said he was sorry he missed them and the cook came to the door then and said dinner was ready and Mama asked him if he would have dinner with us and he said no, he didn't want to put us out any and Mama said you're not putting anybody out and I insist you eat with us and he said well, if you insist and we went in the dining room. We had a roast, as I remember, rice and gravy, fresh black-eye peas, okra and molded salad, and I never saw anybody eat the way he did. Talking all the while, too. He said did we know he had been given custody of the three children and Lenora had been declared by the courts an unfit mother and had we heard that? We said no we hadn't and Brother and Cornelia came in from the country then and joined us at the table and Mama said Mr. Davis, did you know my oldest girl Beth is dead? Been dead ten years and he said I was indeed aware of that sad event and of your husband's death too, and please don't call me Mr. Davis, call me Leon. He'd had three helpings of everything by then and he was telling us about the insurance company he was starting in Houston, and that he had been in Victoria talking to potential investors. He stayed for another hour and then said goodbye. Leon Davis began stopping by every two or three days after that.

Always, he said, on his way to or from Victoria. He told us one afternoon what happened when he killed our Uncle. He explained why he had been acquitted. He said the butcher knife our Uncle tried to stab him with was lethal and then he showed us a picture of his three children and I must say they were very sweet-looking and he seemed devoted to them. Then Mama said Sissie sing the song you were singing when your Papa died and I said Mama I can't ever sing that song again; it's too upsetting to me. Then Mama proceeded to tell Mr. Davis all about my singing when Papa died and how I began to scream and they all came running in including the cook and we were all screaming then, and Mama said Sissie please sing that song just one more time for Mr. Davis and he said Leon, remember, and she said, I'm sorry, Leon. Please Sissie sing, "O, the Clanging Bells of Time" just once more so Leon can hear it. I know by now you might as well let Mama have her way or she'll drive you crazy trying to get it. So, I gave in: *(In the distance we can hear Sissie singing, then Sissie begins to sing, too, as the offstage voice fades away.)*

"O, the clanging bells of time,
Night and day they never cease;
We are wearied with their chime,
For they do not bring us peace;
And we hush our breath to hear,
And we strain our eyes to see;
If thy shores are drawing near,
Eternity! Eternity!"

It was about that time that Brother came in with Mrs. Carpenter and when Mama saw her she began to holler get that hussy out of here and carried on so poor Mrs. Carpenter and Brother had to leave, and after we quieted Mama down, she turned to Mr. Davis and said, Did you hear about my daughter Beth? She passed away ten years ago today. Mama, I said, she didn't pass away ten years ago and it wasn't on this day. Mama looked at me like I was crazy and Cornelia said.

CORNELIA. Mr. Davis.

SISSIE. *(Imitating Leon.)* Please, please, call me Leon.

CORNELIA. I'm sorry, Leon. How is your insurance business coming along?

SISSIE. Splendid, he said. And off he went talking so fast, I couldn't hardly understand a thing he said, but to tell you the truth if he had been talking slow I couldn't have understood any of it, for I have no head at all for figures, just none and I looked over at Cornelia and she was listening to everything he said and nodding her head like she approved of his every word and every figure and I thought to myself Cornelia is smitten with him, and then Mama turned to me and said would you sing the song you were singing when your Papa died for Mr. Davis? Leon, remember, Leon, he said. I'm sorry Mama said, what was the name of that song, Sissie? "O, the Clanging Bells of Time," I said. That's right. Sing it for Mr. Davis. Leon, he said. I'm sorry, Mama said, Leon. I just sang it for him, Mama. You heard me. Well, sing it again. It comforts me. Wouldn't you like to hear it again, Mr. Davis? Leon, Leon, he said. Sorry Mr. Leon, Mama said. Not Mr. Leon, just Leon, he said. Sing it, honey, Mama said. One more time. Go ahead and sing it, Sissie, Cornelia said, she'll give us no peace until you do. And so I sang it. *(Again in the distance we hear "O, the Clanging Bells of Time." Sissie listens as if remembering the song. The song is prerecorded.)* Mama began to sing along with me. Then Leon joined in on the eternities. *(And she listens as if remembering hearing her mother and Leon join her in singing. This is all prerecorded.)* And Brother came in then and he said Jackson Le Grand is dead he was sitting on a stool at the drugstore and he just keeled over. Which drugstore? Mama asked and Brother said he forgot to ask, and she said to me; Sissie call Grace Anne and ask her which drugstore it was, and I said I'm not going to do that Mama, and Brother said I think somebody should call over and see how Grace Anne is. I'll call, Cornelia said, and she did and she came back and said she's holding up pretty well, both her girls have been notified in Houston and are taking the next train home. Maybe I should take the car and meet them, Brother said. I think that would be nice. I said. And maybe we should offer to pay for the funeral. I don't think they have a dime left. Jackson Le Grand was no businessman and certainly no cotton farmer. After Brother left for the station everybody got real quiet, thinking their own thoughts. And then I said to Mama, Do you think Grace Anne will start speaking to Brother again now? I asked. Why doesn't she speak to him? Mama wanted to know. Now you know why, Mama, I said. I do not, she said. If I ever knew I've forgotten. Grace Anne heard that Brother said that Jackson married her for her money and Brother said he thought he had and she said he had to go to people he said it to and say he was mistaken and he refused and she said unless he did she would never speak to him again. Well, she did start speaking to him again, and I must say Brother was a rock. He made all the funeral arrangements for her, all of which the Estate paid for and they had Jackson Le Grand on view at their house for two days before the funeral and Brother insisted on sitting up with his body both nights so Grace Anne could get some sleep, and Cornelia and I went downtown and bought suitable dresses for Grace Anne and the girls to wear at the funeral, and Cornelia offered to have people come back to our house after the service since the living room of our house was three times the size of their living room, and Grace Anne thanked her but said she'd rather see people in her own house and that's what she did. After the cemetery Mama went back with us to Grace Anne's house and I must say the neighbors and friends sent in delicious food and in the middle of it all Mama turned to me and said Sissie sing "O, the Clanging Bells of Time." I had been a little hurt to tell you the truth that Grace Anne hadn't asked me to sing at Jackson's funeral, but instead asked Pansy Fullmore who always sings off key. Pansy was sitting next to me in Grace Anne's living room and to get Mama off the subject of my singing I said Pansy I thought you sang wonderfully today. Oh, thank you, she said, but Mama wouldn't give up and she kept after me to sing "O, the Clanging Bells of Time" and I looked over at Cornelia and Grace Anne and they both said to me to please sing it and get it over with and so I did. Mama joining in again. *(The lights fade as we hear prerecorded Sissie and her mother singing, "O, the Clanging Bells of Time." The lights are brought up on Grace Anne's area. Grace Anne is sewing.)*

GRACE ANNE. Brother and I finally made up, after Jackson died, and it was a relief to me. He came over real often then. He couldn't take Mrs. Carpenter over to Mama's house because of the way Mama carried on when she saw them together and so Brother started bringing her over here and we had nice visits together.

Brother was all excited that he might get a job with Leon Davis when he started his insurance company. He said if he had any money of his own he would invest in it, because it was going to make somebody rich. He said he was trying to get Cornelia to invest for the Estate, and she wanted to, but Leon wouldn't accept her money because he said he wouldn't sleep nights feeling so responsible. Why if anything happened and he lost her money he would never forgive himself. Brother said he thought Leon was sweet on Cornelia and he thought she liked him too. Leon was there almost every day and Mama was crazy about him too and Sissie and Sissie's little girl called him Uncle Leon. Brother came over by himself the other afternoon and said he had decided when he got his job with the insurance company he was going to marry Mrs. Carpenter. He didn't care what Mama would say, he said he had already asked Mrs. Carpenter if they married would she sign an agreement not to ever sue for part of the Estate like my husband and I did, and he said Mrs. Carpenter would gladly agree to that. Then Leon agreed to let Cornelia invest in his company and it was to be done in three payments — fifteen thousand dollars each. She gave him the first payment on a Friday and Leon on that day told Brother he now had a job and he was going to have an office in Victoria and Houston and which office would he like to be in? And Brother said let me ask Mrs. Carpenter where she would like to live, because we're going to be married, and Leon asked him when and he said as soon as I can get the license and I'd like you to be my best man and Leon said he'd be honored and where would the ceremony take place in a church? Brother said no he was going to ask me if they could be married at my house, which he did and I said he certainly could. Then he came over and Mama was raising a fit about his marrying and said she wouldn't have Mrs. Carpenter in her house married or not and he said after the wedding could they stay with me until he found a place for them to live in Houston when he started work for Leon Davis and I said they certainly could and he said he would pay rent for as long as he stayed and I thanked him and I said that would certainly be a help to me, as I had decided next year to get in a little extra income to rent my spare room to a school teacher now that my girls were grown and living in Houston. And I asked Brother

if Mrs. Carpenter had any family that would be coming for the wedding and he said no that both her parents were dead and she was an only child. I then asked him if he was going to have anybody in town to the wedding and he said no he wanted it small and intimate and he would just have his three sisters and Mama if she would come and Leon Davis who was going to be his best man and maybe I could be the matron of honor and I said I thought I best not as I had turned down Sissie when my feelings were still hurt over Papa's treatment of Jackson. Anyway, it turned out that Mama wouldn't come, but Sissie agreed to sing, "Oh, Promise Me" and Cornelia ordered flowers for the house so the living room looked real pretty and festive. Now Mrs. Carpenter was a Baptist and Brother was a Methodist, although neither of them ever went to church except at Easter and Christmas, so they decided to ask the Episcopalian minister to marry them and he accepted. We decided to have the wedding at twelve noon and Cornelia said she would bring food to eat after the ceremony and Brother told me for their honeymoon Cornelia said the Estate was paying for a weekend at a hotel of their choice in Houston. At ten o'clock Sissie and her girl and Cornelia came with the flowers and the food Cornelia had prepared. Cornelia is the big Boss now you know just like Beth used to be, but I don't say anything. I just let her take over even if it is my house, and while Cornelia was busy arranging flowers Sissie came over to me and said —
SISSIE. *(Whispering.)* We may be having another wedding soon.
GRACE ANNE. Who is that going to be?
SISSIE. *(Whispering.)* Cornelia and Leon Davis, but don't say a word about it until she tells you.
GRACE ANNE. How do you know about it? Did Cornelia tell you?
SISSIE. No. I heard Leon ask Mama's permission to marry her.
GRACE ANNE. Is he going to sign an agreement like your husband did and Mrs. Carpenter has done? But before she could tell me all of it Mrs. Carpenter came in all dressed up for the wedding and you've heard I'm sure that saying all brides are beautiful, but I must say in Mrs. Carpenter's case it was true, as I always thought she was attractive and pleasant enough looking but nothing to write home about but I'll have to say on this day she was just lovely looking. Then Brother came in and Mama. I almost

dropped over dead when I saw Mama, but I didn't act surprised at all. I thought Mrs. Carpenter looked scared to death like she had no idea now what to expect, whether to go on over and speak to Mama or run out of the room. Finally, I saw her take a deep breath and go over to Mama and say hello. Mama looked at her like she had never seen her before in her life and then Brother said Mama you remember Mrs. Carpenter and Mama looked her down and said, is she the one you are up and marrying? Yes, Mama, Brother said. Well, I wish you both happiness she said and then she looked around the room and said where is Leon? And Brother said he's on his way Mama, the wedding isn't until twelve and then Mama said where is Cornelia?

CORNELIA. I'm here, Mama.

GRACE ANNE. Did she tell you her news? Mama said. Leon Davis asked her to marry him.

CORNELIA. Mama. *(She starts to the table in the center of the stage and sits.)*

GRACE ANNE. Nothing makes me happier, Cornelia, Mama said. I'm fond of Leon Davis. Brother said all we need now is my best man who'll be here in two minutes and we can get started. *(Grace Anne, too, sits at the center table. The lights are brought up on Sissie's area.)*

SISSIE. Well, he wasn't there in two minutes, nor in five, nor in ten, nor in twenty, nor in thirty. I hope he's all right, I said, I hope he hasn't had an accident. Where is he coming from? The Episcopalian minister asked. Houston, Brother said. What are we waiting for Mama kept asking every five minutes. Leon, Brother kept telling her. When forty minutes had passed Cornelia said I'll call his apartment. She went into the next room then and we waited another five minutes and she came back out. No one answered the phone, she said. I guess we'd better get started Brother said. I'll have to be my own best man. Everybody sat down and I went to the piano and I began to sing "Oh, Promise Me" *(Again it's Sissie's memory of her singing the song and we hear it continuing all through her speech. Again the song is prerecorded.)* And Grace Anne began to cry in the middle of the song and I looked over at Cornelia and she looked like death I thought, but she wasn't crying and I looked at my daughter and at Mama and Mrs. Carpenter and I heard a car come down the street and I said a prayer to myself please God let it be Leon Davis, but before I could ever finish my prayer I heard the car pass Grace Anne's house and head on into town. I finished singing then and the Episcopalian minister nodded to Brother and Mrs. Carpenter and they all went to the front of the room and the Preacher or Pastor or Father or whatever they call the minister of the Episcopalian Church was about to begin the services when Cornelia let out a sob and ran out of the room. Where's Cornelia going? Mama asked. Sh, Mama, I said. Don't sh me she said. I want to know where Cornelia is going? Maybe home, Mama, I said. I don't think she's feeling too well. What's wrong with her? Mama asked. Never mind, Mama, I said. She'll be all right. How do you know? Mama, Brother said, may we please go on with the service? I'm worried about Cornelia, Mama said. I'll go see to her Mama, I said. I want to go with you. All right, come on, and I took her out of the house. Then Grace Anne told me later that the Preacher waited a minute until they heard my car start and go down the road and then he went on with the service. It was all very sad as you can imagine. As far as any of us knew Cornelia never heard a word from Leon Davis, nor did she ever see a penny of that fifteen thousand dollars again. She never discussed any of it with me ever, nor did I expect her to, and Grace Anne said she never mentioned it to her either, nor did she to Brother until one day she called him into her office at the house and showed him a newspaper clipping from a San Diego, California paper. It was an account of Leon Davis' death. Who sent that to you? Brother asked. She handed him the envelope and he saw there was no name and no return address on it, and there was nothing inside the envelope but the clipping. The Second World War came along about then and the town was often filled with Soldiers and German prisoners of War were brought in and kept at the Fair Grounds and we used to get in our car and ride out and look at them, now and again. The street around our house began changing, getting more and more commercial. Filling stations and fast food restaurants and used car lots until finally our house was the only one left. Cornelia had a chance to sell it for commercial property but she refused. Cotton farming began to change after the War and the cotton picking machines and tractors began to replace the wagons and mules and tenant farmers and their families. Brother said it seemed to him there was nothing for Cornelia to do but change with the times and she finally agreed. She decided she had to then go out and tell the tenants and their wives and their children that had been on the land, some of them thirty or forty years, none of them less than ten, that they had to leave. Brother went with her and he said it almost killed her to have to tell these people they had to move and find another place as she could no longer afford to farm in the old way. It was all very depressing but I didn't let it get me down. Whenever I got worried or depressed, I would just sing to myself "Brighten the Corner." *(Sissie sings as she goes to her chair and the light fades. The lights are brought up on Grace Anne's area.)*

GRACE ANNE. Sissie died. She went to sleep one night and never woke up. Sissie's daughter went to live with her father in Houston and Cornelia was alone in that big old house with just Mama. Once in a while Cornelia would bring Mama over to see me and Mama was talking all the time now about Beth and Papa and Sissie like they were still alive. She had Papa now a General in the Union Army and that he had been invited by the town of Harrison to come in after the Civil War to bring order to the town and to the county. She had it now they had given him several medals for his service to the town and the county. When I asked her where the medals were she said she had given them to Leon Davis to keep for her and he'd be bringing them back one day. Cornelia just shook her head and sighed at that. She goes on like this sometimes day and night she said. She is wearing me out. I think I'm going to have to hire a colored woman to come in and stay with her. I don't blame you at all I told her. A week later Brother told me Cornelia had hired two colored women to stay with Mama. One in the day time and one at night. That Fall during cotton season I rode out to the farms to see the cotton picking machines at work. I had never seen one before. It was quite a sight, and can you believe it, in all these years I had never seen any of Papa's farms before? It's beautiful land. Best in the county, Brother said. *(She begins her sewing again as the lights fade. The lights are brought up on Cornelia's area. In the distance we hear cars and an occasional truck pass.)*

CORNELIA. I have two very refined and lovely colored ladies

staying with Mama. One of them is Rosa Gilbert who is very religious and reads the book of Psalms all the time. She has begun reading them aloud to Mama and it seems to calm her. She doesn't talk constantly about the past the way she used to. She told Rosa Gilbert one day about Papa being a General in the Union Army and then she told her he had personally sent for some Quakers to come here to teach the children of the slaves after the War to read and write and because of that the Ku Klux Klan threatened to burn our house down and if it hadn't been for his friend Colonel Hawkins it might have happened. But Colonel Hawkins stood guard over our house with his gun one night and frightened the Ku Klux Klan away. I told Rosa of course that it might be true, but I doubt it as I'd never heard Papa speak of it. *(She pulls a box from under her chair and opens it.)* Anyway, I decided then to go up to the attic where Sissie used to play paper dolls with her friends when it rained and look in a trunk that had some of Papa's things stored away. I found Papa's discharge papers from the Union Army. He was a Private and I found some old canceled checks and bills of sale for the land he had bought all those years ago and found his Army uniform. *(She takes the uniform from the box.)* I showed it to Mama and said, Mama, see Papa was only a Private but she spit at me and ordered me out of the room. *(She puts the uniform aside and gets out of the chair.)* I don't know how much longer I can go on. Farming is getting so expensive now. I promised Papa I would never sell off the land, and I never have except for that time with Grace Anne and Jackson Le Grand and fortunately I was able to buy that back. And I certainly don't want to sell now, although who am I holding on to it for? Sissie is dead. Grace Anne? How much longer will she be here? She's five years older than I am. Brother? He's seven years older. Mama? Sissie's daughter or Grace Anne's girls? Sissie said her daughter told her if the land was hers she would sell it in a minute and I expect she would. *(A pause.)* It almost killed me the day I had to go out and tell the tenants I had to change how I was farming or I'd lose everything. I don't know whether they believed me or not. Old Jake Tillman and his wife had been on their place nearly forty years and his daddy ten years before him, anyway they cried and I cried when I told them the fix I was in. Some of the others just didn't look at me while I was talking to them. Just stared down at their feet and I couldn't even see their faces. They all said they understood, but I'm not sure they did. I gave each of them a little money and six months grace to relocate. *(A pause.)* I got a letter with no address or name on the envelope with just a clipping inside saying Leon Davis had died. I'll go to my grave wondering who sent me that clipping. I didn't tell anybody not even Brother, but a year after Leon Davis disappeared I called my cousin Lenora who was his wife and I asked her if she knew where he was and she asked me why, does he owe you money? If he does she said, you'll never get it. He owes everybody in the city of Houston. He got a lot of fools to invest in some scheme he had about an insurance company and once he got their money he just disappeared. What about the children? What about the children? She said. Didn't he have custody of them? Who told you that lie? He's never gone near his children since he killed Papa all those years ago. Never sent them a dime either. *(A pause. She points to the plaque behind her.)* Did you see the plaque the Historical Society is putting up on our house? We're the oldest house in town now. There used to be ten or fifteen older some right on this street but they were all sold off long ago and replaced by filling stations and God knows what all. Oh, well. *(She goes to the table and picks up a document.)* The plaque reads: The Joseph Thompson house built in 1870 by Joseph Thompson, a Soldier in the Union Army has been listed in the National Register of Historic Places by the United States Department of the Interior. I showed it to Mama and she said they have it wrong. He wasn't in the Union Army, he was in the Confederate Army and he was General and he was wounded at the Battle of Shiloh. I thought, well, tomorrow she'll go back to his being a General in the Union Army, but at breakfast the first thing she said to me was are you gonna have that lie changed about his being in the Union Army? There are a group of people coming over here to celebrate the placing of the plaque on our house. And they asked me if I would have Mama here to say a few words to them about Papa and the history of the house, and I said that would not be possible and they would have to settle for me or my Brother or Grace Anne, for I knew if Mama got out here she would go on about his being a General in the Union Army or the

Confederate Army and the Ku Klux Klan and God knows what all. Brother and his wife and Grace Anne will come over and I've made some coffee and will serve that and fruitcake to the guests after the ceremony. *(Traffic noises are heard.)* Hear that traffic? It gets worse all the time. It used to be so quiet here. When Beth was sick and we brought her home to die the men in the town covered the street with straw so there'd be no noise when the wagons and the horses went by. I wonder what they would have to do now to stop the noise. I wonder sometimes about Beth. Did we do the right thing in telling her she was going to be all right? *(In the distance we hear Mrs. Thompson calling: Cornelia. Cornelia. Cornelia.)* That's Mama calling me. I know what she wants. Mama is going to ask me to get Sissie to sing, "O, the Clanging Bells of Time," and there is no sense in telling her Sissie is dead because she won't believe me, and the only way to shut her up is to go in the next room and pretend I'm Sissie and sing it for her, pitiful voice that I have. *(She goes to her chair and picks up the uniform and slowly starts across the stage singing "O, the Clanging Bells of Time.")*

"O, the clanging bells of time,
Night and day they never cease;
We are wearied with their chime,
For they do not bring us peace;
And we hush our breath to hear,
And we strain our eyes to see;
If thy shores are drawing near,

(And Grace Anne and Sissie join her in Eternity.)

Eternity! Eternity!"

(As the lights go down and the stage is in darkness.)

End of Play

PROPERTY LIST

Ledger book and pen (CORNELIA)
Dress fabric, needle, thread, other sewing things, etc. (GRACE ANNE)
Sheet music (SISSIE)
Box containing an army uniform (CORNELIA)
Document (CORNELIA)

SOUND EFFECTS

Dance music
In the distance, a child faintly singing "Jesus Loves Me"
In the distance, Sissie singing, "O, the Clanging Bells of Time"
In the distance, Sissie and Mama singing "O, the Clanging Bells of Time"
In the distance, the sounds of cars and trucks passing
More traffic noises
In the distance, Mama calling, "Cornelia. Cornelia. Cornelia."

NEW PLAYS

★ **THE CREDEAUX CANVAS by Keith Bunin.** A forged painting leads to tragedy among friends. "There is that moment between adolescence and middle age when being disaffected looks attractive. Witness the enduring appeal of Prince Hamlet, Jake Barnes and James Dean, on the stage, page and screen. Or, more immediately, take a look at the lithe young things in THE CREDEAUX CANVAS..." *–NY Times.* "THE CREDEAUX CANVAS is the third recent play about painters...it turned out to be the best of the lot, better even than most plays about non-painters." *–NY Magazine.* [2M, 2W] ISBN: 0-8222-1838-0

★ **THE DIARY OF ANNE FRANK by Frances Goodrich and Albert Hackett, newly adapted by Wendy Kesselman.** A transcendently powerful new adaptation in which Anne Frank emerges from history a living, lyrical, intensely gifted young girl. "Undeniably moving. It shatters the heart. The evening never lets us forget the inhuman darkness waiting to claim its incandescently human heroine." *–NY Times.* "A sensitive, stirring and thoroughly engaging new adaptation." *–NY Newsday.* "A powerful new version that moves the audience to gasps, then tears." *–A.P.* "One of the year's ten best." *–Time Magazine.* [5M, 5W, 3 extras] ISBN: 0-8222-1718-X

★ **THE BOOK OF LIZ by David Sedaris and Amy Sedaris.** Sister Elizabeth Donderstock makes the cheese balls that support her religious community, but feeling unappreciated among the Squeamish, she decides to try her luck in the outside world. "...[a] delightfully off-key, off-color hymn to clichés we all live by, whether we know it or not." *–NY Times.* "Good-natured, goofy and frequently hilarious..." *–NY Newsday.* "...[THE BOOK OF LIZ] may well be the world's first Amish picaresque...hilarious..." *–Village Voice.* [2M, 2W (doubling, flexible casting to 8M, 7W)] ISBN: 0-8222-1827-5

★ **JAR THE FLOOR by Cheryl L. West.** A quartet of black women spanning four generations makes up this hilarious and heartwarming dramatic comedy. "...a moving and hilarious account of a black family sparring in a Chicago suburb..." *–NY Magazine.* "...heart-to-heart confrontations and surprising revelations...first-rate..." *–NY Daily News.* "...unpretentious good feelings...bubble through West's loving and humorous play..." *–Star-Ledger.* "...one of the wisest plays I've seen in ages...[from] a master playwright." *–USA Today.* [5W] ISBN: 0-8222-1809-7

★ **THIEF RIVER by Lee Blessing.** Love between two men over decades is explored in this incisive portrait of coming to terms with who you are. "Mr. Blessing unspools the plot ingeniously, skipping back and forth in time as the details require...an absorbing evening." *–NY Times.* "...wistful and sweet-spirited..." *–Variety.* [6M] ISBN: 0-8222-1839-9

★ **THE BEGINNING OF AUGUST by Tom Donaghy.** When Jackie's wife abruptly and mysteriously leaves him and their infant daughter, a pungently comic reevaluation of suburban life ensues. "Donaghy holds a cracked mirror up to the contemporary American family, anatomizing its frailties and miscommunications in fractured language that can be both funny and poignant." *–The Philadelphia Inquirer.* "...[A] sharp, eccentric new comedy. Pungently funny...fresh and precise..." *–LA Times.* [3M, 2W] ISBN: 0-8222-1786-4

★ **OUTSTANDING MEN'S MONOLOGUES 2001–2002 and OUTSTANDING WOMEN'S MONOLOGUES 2001–2002 edited by Craig Pospisil.** Drawn exclusively from Dramatists Play Service publications, these collections for actors feature over fifty monologues each and include an enormous range of voices, subject matter and characters. MEN'S ISBN: 0-8222-1821-6 WOMEN'S ISBN: 0-8222-1822-4

NEW PLAYS

★ **A LESSON BEFORE DYING by Romulus Linney, based on the novel by Ernest J. Gaines.** An innocent young man is condemned to death in backwoods Louisiana and must learn to die with dignity. "The story's wrenching power lies not in its outrage but in the almost inexplicable grace the characters must muster as their only resistance to being treated like lesser beings." *–The New Yorker.* "Irresistable momentum and a cathartic explosion...a powerful inevitability." *–NY Times.* [5M, 2W] ISBN: 0-8222-1785-6

★ **BOOM TOWN by Jeff Daniels.** A searing drama mixing small-town love, politics and the consequences of betrayal. "...a brutally honest, contemporary foray into classic themes, exploring what moves people to lie, cheat, love and dream. By BOOM TOWN's climactic end there are no secrets, only bare truth." *–Oakland Press.* "...some of the most electrifying writing Daniels has ever done..." *–Ann Arbor News.* [2M, 1W] ISBN: 0-8222-1760-0

★ **INCORRUPTIBLE by Michael Hollinger.** When a motley order of medieval monks learns their patron saint no longer works miracles, a larcenous, one-eyed minstrel shows them an outrageous new way to pay old debts. "A lightning-fast farce, rich in both verbal and physical humor." *–American Theatre.* "Everything fits snugly in this funny, endearing black comedy...an artful blend of the mock-formal and the anachronistically breezy...A piece of remarkably dexterous craftsmanship." *–Philadelphia Inquirer.* "A farcical romp, scintillating and irreverent." *–Philadelphia Weekly.* [5M, 3W] ISBN: 0-8222-1787-2

★ **CELLINI by John Patrick Shanley.** Chronicles the life of the original "Renaissance Man," Benvenuto Cellini, the sixteenth-century Italian sculptor and man-about-town. Adapted from the autobiography of Benvenuto Cellini, translated by J. Addington Symonds. "[Shanley] has created a convincing Cellini, not neglecting his dark side, and a trim, vigorous, fast-moving show." *–BackStage.* "Very entertaining...With brave purpose, the narrative undermines chronology before untangling it...touching and funny..." *–NY Times.* [7M, 2W (doubling)] ISBN: 0-8222-1808-9

★ **PRAYING FOR RAIN by Robert Vaughan.** Examines a burst of fatal violence and its aftermath in a suburban high school. "Thought provoking and compelling." *–Denver Post.* "Vaughan's powerful drama offers hope and possibilities." *–Theatre.com.* "[The play] doesn't put forth compact, tidy answers to the problem of youth violence. What it does offer is a compelling exploration of the forces that influence an individual's choices, and of the proverbial lifelines—be they familial, communal, religious or political—that tragically slacken when society gives in to apathy, fear and self-doubt..." *–Westword.* "...a symphony of anger..." *–Gazette Telegraph.* [4M, 3W] ISBN: 0-8222-1807-0

★ **GOD'S MAN IN TEXAS by David Rambo.** When a young pastor takes over one of the most prestigious Baptist churches from a rip-roaring old preacher-entrepreneur, all hell breaks loose. "...the pick of the litter of all the works at the Humana Festival..." *–Providence Journal.* "...a wealth of both drama and comedy in the struggle for power..." *–LA Times.* "...the first act is so funny...deepens in the second act into a sobering portrait of fear, hope and self-delusion..." *–Columbus Dispatch.* [3M] ISBN: 0-8222-1801-1

★ **JESUS HOPPED THE 'A' TRAIN by Stephen Adly Guirgis.** A probing, intense portrait of lives behind bars at Rikers Island. "...fire-breathing...whenever it appears that JESUS is settling into familiar territory, it slides right beneath expectations into another, fresher direction. It has the courage of its intellectual restlessness...[JESUS HOPPED THE 'A' TRAIN] has been written in flame." *–NY Times.* [4M, 1W] ISBN: 0-8222-1799-6

NEW PLAYS

★ **THE CIDER HOUSE RULES, PARTS 1 & 2 by Peter Parnell, adapted from the novel by John Irving.** Spanning eight decades of American life, this adaptation from the Irving novel tells the story of Dr. Wilbur Larch, founder of the St. Cloud's, Maine orphanage and hospital, and of the complex father-son relationship he develops with the young orphan Homer Wells. "…luxurious digressions, confident pacing…an enterprise of scope and vigor…" *–NY Times.* "…The fact that I can't wait to see Part 2 only begins to suggest just how good it is…" *–NY Daily News.* "…engrossing…an odyssey that has only one major shortcoming: It comes to an end." *–Seattle Times.* "…outstanding…captures the humor, the humility…of Irving's 588-page novel…" *–Seattle Post-Intelligencer.* [9M, 10W, doubling, flexible casting] PART 1 ISBN: 0-8222-1725-2 PART 2 ISBN: 0-8222-1726-0

★ **TEN UNKNOWNS by Jon Robin Baitz.** An iconoclastic American painter in his seventies has his life turned upside down by an art dealer and his ex-boyfriend. "…breadth and complexity…a sweet and delicate harmony rises from the four cast members…Mr. Baitz is without peer among his contemporaries in creating dialogue that spontaneously conveys a character's social context and moral limitations…" *–NY Times.* "…darkly funny, brilliantly desperate comedy…TEN UNKNOWNS vibrates with vital voices." *–NY Post.* [3M, 1W] ISBN: 0-8222-1826-7

★ **BOOK OF DAYS by Lanford Wilson.** A small-town actress playing St. Joan struggles to expose a murder. "…[Wilson's] best work since *Fifth of July*…An intriguing, prismatic and thoroughly engrossing depiction of contemporary small-town life with a murder mystery at its core…a splendid evening of theater…" *–Variety.* "…fascinating…a densely populated, unpredictable little world." *–St. Louis Post-Dispatch.* [6M, 5W] ISBN: 0-8222-1767-8

★ **THE SYRINGA TREE by Pamela Gien.** Winner of the 2001 Obie Award. A breathtakingly beautiful tale of growing up white in apartheid South Africa. "Instantly engaging, exotic, complex, deeply shocking…a thoroughly persuasive transport to a time and a place…stun[s] with the power of a gut punch…" *–NY Times.* "Astonishing…affecting …[with] a dramatic and heartbreaking conclusion…A deceptive sweet simplicity haunts THE SYRINGA TREE…" *–A.P.* [1W (or flexible cast)] ISBN: 0-8222-1792-9

★ **COYOTE ON A FENCE by Bruce Graham.** An emotionally riveting look at capital punishment. "The language is as precise as it is profane, provoking both troubling thought and the occasional cheerful laugh…will change you a little before it lets go of you." *–Cincinnati CityBeat.* "…excellent theater in every way…" *–Philadelphia City Paper.* [3M, 1W] ISBN: 0-8222-1738-4

★ **THE PLAY ABOUT THE BABY by Edward Albee.** Concerns a young couple who have just had a baby and the strange turn of events that transpire when they are visited by an older man and woman. "An invaluable self-portrait of sorts from one of the few genuinely great living American dramatists…rockets into that special corner of theater heaven where words shoot off like fireworks into dazzling patterns and hues." *–NY Times.* "An exhilarating, wicked…emotional terrorism." *–NY Newsday.* [2M, 2W] ISBN: 0-8222-1814-3

★ **FORCE CONTINUUM by Kia Corthron.** Tensions among black and white police officers and the neighborhoods they serve form the backdrop of this discomfiting look at life in the inner city. "The creator of this intense…new play is a singular voice among American playwrights…exceptionally eloquent…" *–NY Times.* "…a rich subject and a wise attitude." *–NY Post.* [6M, 2W, 1 boy] ISBN: 0-8222-1817-8